W9-CSK-007

DATE DUE

GAYLORD

PRINTED IN U.S.A.

Science at the Edge

Alternative Energy Sources

Sally Morgan

Heinemann Library
Chicago, Illinois

Customer Service 888-454-2279

Visit our website at www.heinemannlibrary.com

Designed by Tinstar Design (www.tinstar.co.uk)
Illustrations by Nicholas Beresford-Davies and Jeff Edwards
Originated by Ambassador Litho, Ltd.
Printed and bound in Hong Kong/China by
South China Printing Company, Ltd.

07 06 05 04
10 9 8 7 6 5 4 3

Library of Congress Cataloging-in-Publication Data
Morgan, Sally.
  Alternative energy sources / Sally Morgan.
    v. cm. -- (Science at the edge)
Contents: Fossil fuelled world -- Generating electricity -- Storing
energy -- Harnessing the wind -- Trapping light -- Hydro power --
Geothermal power -- Nuclear energy -- Biopower -- The future of
renewable sources -- Summary spread -- Time line.
Includes index.
 ISBN 1-40340-322-8
 1. Renewable energy sources--Juvenile literature. [1. Renewable energy
sources. 2. Power resources.] I. Title. II. Series.
  TJ808.2 .M67 2002
  333.79'4--dc21

Acknowledgments
The author and publishers are grateful to the following for permission to reproduce copyright material:
p. 5 Dan Chung/Popperfoto/Reuters; p. 7 Alex Bartel/Science Photo Library; p. 8 Herbert
Girardel/Environmental Images; pp. 10, 48 David Townend/Environmental Images; p. 11 Vanessa
Vick/Science Photo Library; pp. 13, 49 Joel Creed/Ecoscene; p.15/Science Photo Library; p. 17 Mike
Blake/Popperfoto/Reuters; Middelgrunden Vindmollelaug p20/Environmental Picture Library; pp. 21, 32,
36 Martin Bond/Science Photo Library; pp. 22, 28 Martin Bond/Environmental Images; p. 24
Popperfoto/Reuters; p. 25 Peter Menzel/Science Photo Library; p.27 Popperfoto; p.29 Environmental
Picture Library/Jimmy Holmes; p. 31 NASA; p. 33 Michael Marchant /Environmental Images; pp. 35, 46,
47, 52 Ecoscene; p. 37 Alexandra Jones/Ecoscene; p. 38 John Mead/Science Photo Library; p. 39 Peter
Hulme/Ecoscene; p. 40 Kevin King/Ecoscene; p. 43 Novosti/Science Photo Library; p. 44 US-DES/Science
Photo Library; p. 45 Los Alamos National Laboratory/Science Photo Library; p. 50 Prof. David
Hall/Science Photo Library; p. 51 Environmental Images; p. 54 Andrew Brown/Ecoscene.

Cover photograph reproduced with permission of Science Photo Library.

Our thanks to Godfrey Boyle for his comments on a draft version of this book.

Every effort has been made to contact copyright holders of any material reproduced in this book.
Any omissions will be rectified in subsequent printings if notice is given to the publishers.

Some words are shown in bold, **like this.** You can find out what they mean by looking
in the glossary.

Contents

Alternative Energy Sources

During 2001, the residents of California discovered what it would be like to live in a world where **electricity** was in short supply. In that year, there were periods of time when the supply could not keep up with the demand, and entire districts had to survive without electricity for many hours. The California crisis was caused by a change in the way power companies sold **energy,** but it was a very good example of how people have become dependent on a regular supply of electricity.

One of the immediate effects of this crisis was that many Californians turned to alternative energy sources. People rushed out and purchased solar panels to provide their homes with electricity and hot water. This gave them independence from the power companies who had traditionally provided their energy.

Run on fossil fuels

The modern world is dependent on **fossil fuels**—oil, gas, coal, and peat. Over the last 200 years or so, the quantities of fossil fuels extracted from the ground have escalated. Fossil fuels are used by power stations to **generate** electricity and fuel cars. They are essential to a modern lifestyle, but they have been used at the expense of the environment. Environmental damage is caused at every stage of extracting, processing, and using these fuels. Coal is mined from the ground, while oil and gas are pumped out of the ground. Then they have to be transported around the world to where they will be used. Finally, when they are burned, these fuels release polluting gases into the atmosphere and cause **acid rain** and **global warming.**

The supply of fossil fuels will eventually run out. Estimates of how long these fuels will last are uncertain, as new deposits are found all the time. However, most experts agree that oil and gas will probably last between 30 and 50 years, while coal may last 200 years.

New energy sources

Over the last 100 years, people have learned how to use the energy locked in fossil fuels. But there are other sources of energy. Each day, vast amounts of solar energy reach the ground. This energy is spread over the whole surface of the planet. The same is true for wind and wave energy. These forms of energy are more difficult and more expensive to use than fossil fuels. However, when fossil fuels start to run out, people will need to find ways of using the energy from these **renewable** sources. At some point in the future, the world's energy needs will probably have to come from these sources.

In September 2000, people in Britain protested the high price of fuel and the tax on gas by blocking oil refineries and storage depots. Gasoline tanker drivers were reluctant to break the blockade, so the British public experienced oil shortages.

A Fossil-Fueled World

Although there are many different sources of **energy** available, more than three-quarters of the energy used in industrialized countries comes from oil, gas, and coal. These fuels are rich in carbon and hydrogen. They burn in air to form carbon dioxide and water, a process that releases heat energy.

Fossil fuel supplies

Fossil fuels were formed millions of years ago from the remains of plants and animals. There is a limited supply of these fuels, and now they are being used up at a far faster rate than they are being formed. Soon they will run out.

Drilling for oil

Oil is formed under the sea from the remains of marine life. The oil formation process is similar to that of coal. The remains become buried under layers of sediment, and the resulting high pressure and temperature cause them to turn into a black liquid with a high carbon content. Often, gas forms in the same place as the oil. The liquid oil moves toward the surface and becomes trapped under layers of **impermeable** rock. The pressure builds up as more liquid moves upward.

Coal formation

The process of coal formation starts with a buildup of dead plant matter, which becomes buried in swampy or waterlogged conditions. The lack of oxygen in the ground prevents bacteria from completely breaking down the plant matter. This decaying matter is buried deeper by more plant material and by sediment. These layers press tightly together, causing the pressure and temperature to increase. Gases and liquids escape to the surface, leaving a solid material behind. Peat develops within hundreds of years and contains about 60 percent carbon. Millions of years later, the peat turns into lignite, a low-grade brown coal with 70 percent carbon. Eventually, the lignite turns into anthracite coal. This is a high-quality coal that is 95 percent carbon.

Although oil is formed under the sea, many of the world's oil fields are located on land. This is a result of changes in sea levels and movements in the earth that have uplifted rocks, causing them to lie above water.

The oil and gas are reached by drilling wells, sometimes several miles long, through the overlying rock. When the drill breaks through the rock above the oil, pressure is released, and the oil spurts out of the well. To prevent this from happening, engineers place special valves at the top of the well. When there is not enough pressure to push the oil to the surface, water or gas can be pumped into the well to force the oil out. The crude oil that comes out must be taken to refineries, where it is processed before it is ready for use.

Oil companies are now searching for new oil and gas fields in some of the world's most inhospitable places, such as the frozen ice fields of Siberia and Alaska and the Arctic Ocean. Once all the oil fields are depleted, the energy companies may turn their attention to oil shales. These are rocks that have oil inside them. However, removing oil from rock is very expensive and produces a lot of waste.

A nodding donkey rig pumps oil to the surface in an onshore oil field in California.

Air pollution

Fossil fuels produce a number of **pollutants** when they are burned, in addition to carbon dioxide and water. Coal often contains sulphur, which is released as sulphur dioxide. Sulphur dioxide is one of the chemicals that cause **acid rain.** When gasoline and diesel fuels are burned in engines, gases such as nitrous oxide and carbon monoxide are released.

Smog

The gases and particles from car **exhaust** pipes can create photochemical **smog.** This form of smog is particularly common in hot, dry, sunny cities such as Athens in Greece, Cairo in Egypt, and Mexico City. The car exhaust pipes pump out gases, such as nitrous oxide, carbon monoxide, and ozone, that react together in the sunlight. The result is a smoggy haze over the city.

Los Angeles has suffered badly in the past from smog. The smog was due in part to the exhaust fumes from millions of cars, but the local geography also played a role. The city lies by the coast and is surrounded by mountains. In certain weather conditions, the smoggy air would be trapped over the city, and air quality would fall steadily until atmospheric conditions changed and the smoggy air was replaced by cleaner air. A hazy layer can still be seen over Los Angeles, but the level of pollutants has fallen dramatically due to new legislation and improved pollution control on cars.

Heavy traffic and local industry contribute to the smog that hangs over Cairo in Egypt.

Acid rain

Coal-fired power stations release sulphur dioxide, especially those that burn lignite coal. This gas, together with nitrous oxides from vehicle exhausts, reacts with water in the air to form weak acids. These acids create acid rain. Acid rain has a lower **pH** than normal. It erodes and damages the outsides of buildings and statues, especially those made of limestone.

Acid rain falling on conifer forests in mountainous areas of Scandinavia, North America, and central Europe has caused long-term damage to the trees. The soil becomes more acidic, and this causes toxic compounds such as aluminum to be released. The first signs of damage are a tree's needles turning brown and whole branches dying. Increased acidity in the soil damages trees' roots, and this reduces their ability to take up water and nutrients. The trees become more vulnerable to frost and disease. Eventually, they die.

Lakes are also at risk. The acidic rainwater drains off soils into the lake, causing it to become more acid. Aluminum in the water causes the gills of fish to produce more mucus, and this prevents them from obtaining sufficient oxygen from the water. In extreme cases, all life in the water may die.

Global warming

Burning fossil fuels releases carbon dioxide. Carbon dioxide is described as a greenhouse gas, because it traps heat in the atmosphere. The presence of some greenhouse gases keeps Earth at a temperature of approximately 59°F (15°C), which allows life to survive. A recent increase in the use of fossil fuels has caused the levels of carbon dioxide in the atmosphere to increase, too. More carbon dioxide means that more heat is trapped, and this has caused the average global temperature to rise. This is called **global warming.**

The effects of global warming are uncertain. However, it is likely that the increasing temperatures will disrupt climates around the world, causing some regions to have lower rainfall and others to have more. The warmer temperatures will cause ice caps and glaciers to melt, which, combined with the expansion of water in the ocean, will cause sea levels to rise, flooding low-lying areas that are heavily populated. Extreme weather events such as droughts and storms could also become more common.

Extraction and transport

Every stage in extracting and processing **fossil fuels** can harm the environment. Coal is mined either from the surface, in huge open mines called strip mines, or by underground tunnels. Strip mining eats up acres of countryside and leaves behind huge holes of little use that send dust and other debris into the atmosphere. Lignite is a poor quality coal that is taken from strip mines. When burned, it releases alot of sulphur dioxide, which creates **acid rain.** Mining produces large quantities of waste, which is usually dumped in piles. Water runs off these piles, and the drainage from these areas can carry **pollutants** into rivers and lakes.

Wells are dug into the ground to bring the oil to the surface. There can be local damage from spills, but most of the damage occurs during its transportation. Some of the largest tankers carry up to 500,000 tons of crude oil and many only have a single hull. Any damage to the hull results in an oil spill. In the past, there have been numerous tanker accidents in which hundreds of thousands of tons of crude oil have spilled into the sea. The oil causes widespread damage to local populations of birds, mammals, and invertebrates and also damages

Brown coal, or lignite, is stripped from the ground in central Europe, creating huge holes. Power stations burn the coal. This coal is of poor quality and releases sulphur dioxide, a gas that causes acid rain.

In 1989, the oil tanker *Exxon Valdez* ran aground off the coast of Alaska and ruptured its tanks. The disaster created a huge oil slick and terrible environmental damage. The cleanup operation cost billions of dollars.

coastlines. Large quantities of oil also enter the water every year when tankers clean out their tanks or minor spills occur in ports.

Changes ahead

Energy demands are increasing all the time. Approximately one third of the world's population lives without **electricity,** relying solely on battery power and **kerosene** lamps and candles. Governments want to supply these people with electricity in order to improve their standard of living. To do so would mean building thousands of new power stations in order to greatly increase the current energy **generating** capacity. This would greatly reduce the remaining supplies of fossil fuels and send carbon dioxide emissions soaring out of control.

The way of the future is to use **renewable** sources of energy that provide electricity without causing massive damage to the environment. At the same time, people will have to use fossil fuels more efficiently to ensure that the supply lasts as long as possible. For example, cars will have to travel farther on a gallon of gas and will have to be more **efficient.**

Making and Storing Electricity

The **electricity** generation process involves a number of **energy** changes, regardless of the initial energy source. Traditionally, electricity has been **generated** using **fossil fuels,** especially coal. More recently, power stations have used oil and gas as their source of energy. Oil-fired power stations are common in oil producing countries, such as Indonesia. Gas burns more cleanly and efficiently than coal. It releases half as much carbon dioxide and more than 1,000 times less sulphur dioxide per unit of energy.

Burning fossil fuels in power stations

The heat released from burning fossil fuels is used to boil water, which produces steam. The steam is heated to very high temperatures so that it is at high pressure and can turn huge steam **turbines.** Some of the energy of the steam is transformed into movement, or **kinetic energy,** as the turbines spin. The turbines are connected to the coils of large **generators.** The coils carry a **current** and act as **electromagnets.** As the turbines spin, they produce an electric current in the fixed coils surrounding them. This is fed into a power supply grid and carried to wherever it is needed.

Power stations cannot store surplus electricity, so electricity generation has to match demand. The power companies have to judge how much power will be needed. During periods of hot weather, electricity demand may increase as more people use air conditioning to keep their homes and offices cool. If power companies' estimates are wrong, people may experience power cuts.

Power stations are not very efficient. Between 50 and 70 percent of the energy contained in fossil fuels is wasted. Some of the heat energy heats the surrounding air and escapes through the boiler chimneys. Not all the heat energy locked in the steam can be transferred to the spinning turbines. Although the steam is cooler when it leaves than when it enters the turbines, it is still warm. The steam is carried to the cooling towers, where it cools sufficiently to **condense** back into water. The warm water is then emptied into a nearby river or sea, where it can cause thermal, or heat, pollution. Warm water holds less oxygen than cold water. The addition of a large quantity of warm water can cause animals such as fish to suffocate, as they are unable to extract enough oxygen from the water.

Combined heat and power plants

Some power stations, called combined heat and power plants (CHP), try to make use of waste heat. They transport waste hot water to surrounding businesses and homes to provide heating. There are many such units in Germany, and many small towns benefit from this cheap energy source. However, this is only possible with small and medium-sized power plants that are built close to towns. In many countries, power stations are located in more remote locations, so this energy source is not practical.

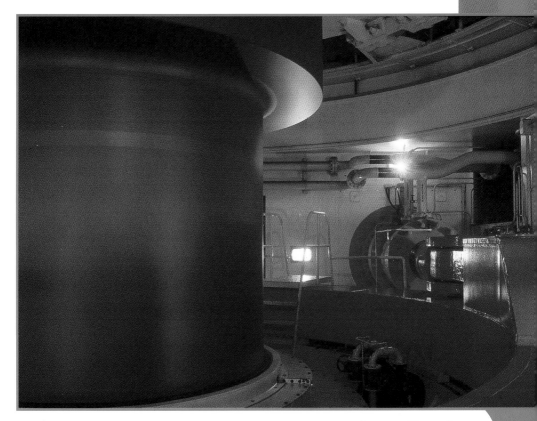

Water is a **renewable** source of energy. The turbine room at the Itaipu Dam in Brazil lies deep inside the dam. The falling water spins the turbines and this, in turn, produces electricity.

Storing energy

Electricity is usually **generated** at a level that meets demand, as it is difficult to store surplus **energy.** However, it is possible to store smaller amounts of energy for personal and domestic uses. Batteries and **fuel cells** both produce electricity by using **electrochemical** reactions. **Flywheels** store energy as they spin.

The battery

A convenient store of energy is the electric cell or battery. These are used every day to power flashlights, radios, toys, and many other appliances. The most common form of battery contains carbon and zinc separated by a solution of ammonium chloride. When the battery is connected to an electrical circuit, its stored chemical energy is changed into electrical energy. The battery continues to produce an electric **current** until all the chemicals have reacted with each other. Then, the battery is said to be flat. Batteries containing nickel and cadmium (Nicads) can be recharged by passing a small electric current through the battery for several hours. This makes them last much longer.

Flywheels

Space stations use **photovoltaic panels** and fuel cells as their source of energy. This energy is stored in batteries. These batteries are large and expensive and have to be replaced every five years. But new space stations and **satellites** may use flywheels to store the energy. These can last up to twenty years. Flywheels are used in engines, but now scientists are designing even more efficient types of flywheels. When energy is used to spin a flywheel, the energy is converted to **kinetic energy.** The flywheel stores the energy mechanically in the form of

Powered by air

When air is pumped into a tire, it becomes compressed and is under great pressure. When the valve is released, the air rushes out with some force. This idea could be used on a much larger scale by power stations. When a power station produces too much electricity, it is usually wasted. Some of this surplus electricity could be used to pump air into underground chambers, such as old salt mines, oil wells, or even natural caves. The surplus electricity would be used to force the air into the chamber under pressure. When the demand for electricity became high, the air could be released to power air-driven **turbines.**

kinetic energy. The faster the flywheel spins, the more energy it stores. This energy can be converted to electricity. Newer flywheels will be just 5.9 inches (15 centimeters) across and will be made of extremely strong yet lightweight materials. They will spin up to 600,000 times each minute and will store eight times more energy than a battery of the same mass.

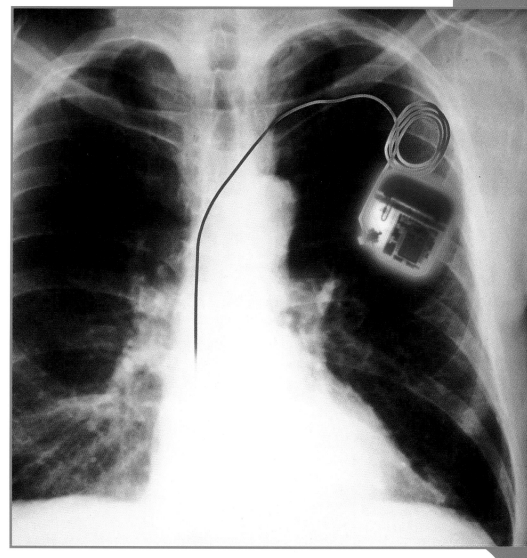

An artificial heart pacemaker is made of titanium and contains a tiny **generator** powered by batteries. These tiny batteries are designed for the very specialized job of keeping the heart beating at the right speed. The pacemaker is inserted under the skin of the chest wall and is connected to the heart. The batteries last a long time and can be changed under local anesthetic.

Fuel cells

In the near future, it is possible that car engines, batteries in laptops, and even power stations could be replaced by **fuel cells.** Fuel cells date back to 1839, but until recently only the National Aeronautics and Space Administration (NASA) used them.

All fuel cells are **energy** converters and work on the same basic principle. They have two **electrodes** separated by an **electrolyte,** a substance that conducts **electricity.** A fuel such as hydrogen enters at one electrode and oxygen enters at the other. They undergo a reaction, which produces an electric **current.** When the fuel is hydrogen, the only waste product is pure water.

Fuel cells have many advantages. They convert energy far more efficiently than conventional power sources. For example, a fuel cell is twice as efficient as a car gas engine and produces virtually no pollution. Furthermore, they contain no moving parts, so they do not produce any noise or vibration. An operating fuel cell is, therefore, very quiet and does not suffer from wear and tear. However, there are a number of problems to overcome. Currently, fuel cells are very costly, although this is due to the fact that only a very few are being manufactured. The price will fall once large quantities are produced. There are also problems of reliability with some fuel cells. In addition, some larger fuel cells have a poor power-to-weight and volume ratio. This means that for their weight or volume, they produce relatively small amounts of power.

> There's no other technology around like fuel cells. They are basically black boxes, you put fuel in one end and get electricity out the other, with great fuel **efficiency** and low emissions.
> Edward Gillis, Electric Power Research Institute, California

Using fuel cells

Fuel cells are already being used in some buses and cars. The fuel cell works with an electric motor that converts the electrical power from the fuel cell into a force to turn the wheels. Buses powered by fuel cells have been tested in Canada, Germany, and the United States. The first fuel cell-powered cars are now appearing. These cars are emission-free and are ideal for places such as California, where there are strict emission laws. Larger systems are being tested in small power stations and houses. A police station in Central Park in New York is using a large fuel cell to provide its electricity and heating. It cost more than one million dollars to install, but this was cheaper than

Fifty cars and buses fitted with fuel cells are currently being evaluated as part of a partnership among technology providers, government agencies, and manufacturers in California, where there are very strict laws concerning **exhaust** emissions from vehicles.

having to lay electricity cables across the park. Hundreds of similar fuel cells have been sold around the world. They are ideal for places that are too remote to be on the national power grid, such as Alaska. Smaller cells are being developed as alternatives to a household boiler.

Hydrogen fuel

Although fuel cells can be run on a number of fuels, the cleanest is hydrogen. Hydrogen can be obtained from a number of sources, including **fossil fuels.** Although this is the most likely source in the short-term, it does not solve the long-term problem of replacing fossil fuels. Hydrogen can also be obtained from organic wastes, which is a **renewable** source. Another method is to split water using a process called electrolysis. This involves passing an electric current through acidic water, which splits it into oxygen and hydrogen. Electrolysis uses a lot of electricity, but in the future this could be **generated** from renewable energy sources, such as wind or solar energy.

Harnessing the Wind

Today there are more than a quarter of a million wind **turbines** around the world. However, only 25 percent of these turbines are used to **generate electricity.** The rest are used to pump water from the ground. Worldwide, wind power has been growing at 30 percent per year and now generates the equivalent of twenty coal-powered power stations. Wind power uses no fuel and does not produce any harmful emissions or wastes, apart from those used in the manufacture of the turbines.

Windy locations

Wind turbines are built where it is windy all the time, such as along coasts and the shores of some large lakes. The modern wind turbine has a tall tower with two or three blades at the top. The blades are moved by the wind. A spinning **generator** directly converts the **kinetic energy** into electricity.

Wind turbine design

Wind turbines come in two basic designs. The key difference is in the drive shaft. This is the part of the turbine that connects the blades to the generator. The most common design is the horizontal axis turbine, with two or three blades. Horizontal axis turbines have a horizontal drive shaft.

Vertical axis turbines have vertical drive shafts. The blades are long and curved and are attached to the tower at the top and bottom. More recently, shrouded wind turbines have appeared. These have a hood around the rotor to funnel the wind over the blades. This causes the wind to move faster over the blades and spin them more quickly.

Wind turbines are increasing in size. The tallest are now more than 394 feet (120 meters) high. The wind is stronger higher above the ground, so taller wind turbines bring the blades into contact with faster moving air. The blades are getting longer too, reaching lengths of 263 feet (80 meters) or more. They are built from light but strong **composite** materials, so they can withstand gusty winds.

The layout

The placing of the wind turbines is also important. If they are placed too close together, they block the wind from neighboring turbines. Computers are used to figure out the best positions. Electronic monitors measure the wind speed and direction. This information is used to adjust the angle of the blades and the direction of the whole turbine to suit the wind conditions. If the blades were allowed to spin too fast, they could break. If the wind is too strong, the blades are either turned out of the wind or brakes are applied.

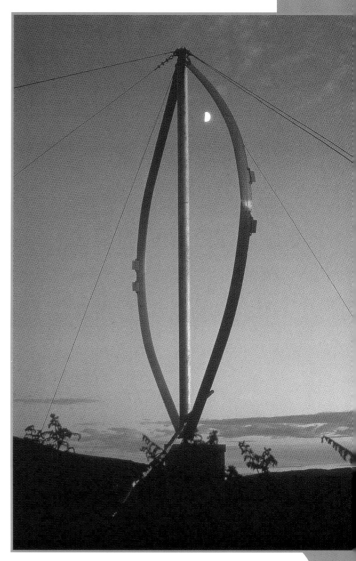

*Our nation's abundant winds can provide a low-cost, clean **energy** solution to the current energy crisis. Wind energy can help power American homes and businesses while providing a buffer against spikes in the price of natural gas and other fuels used to produce electricity in conventional power plants.*
  Randall Swisher, Executive Director, the American Wind Energy Association

Some wind turbines are built with a vertical axis turbine, such as this one in Wales. This type of design is not as popular as horizontal axis turbines, which are used in many places around the world.

Middelgrunden offshore wind farm

The largest offshore wind farm in the world was recently built outside Copenhagen harbor in Denmark. There are twenty wind **generators** there, situated in water between 10 and 16 feet (3 and 5 meters) deep. Each generator is 207 feet (63 meters) tall, with 121-foot (36.8-meter) blades. The generators are 591 feet (180 meters) apart, stretching in an arc for 2 miles (3.4 kilometers). The turbines generate enough **electricity** to power three percent of the city's **energy** needs each year.

Before the wind farm was constructed, the power company did an environmental impact assessment. The farm was to be built on a former dump site for harbor waste, so the area was already classified as unclean. The assessment evaluated what effect the wind farm would have on bird and fish populations, what impact the dredging and construction operation would have, and what the visual impact would be. It was concluded that there would be no adverse impact on the area. It is estimated that the wind farm will result in annual savings of 258 tons of sulphur dioxide, 76,000 tons of carbon dioxide, 231 tons of nitrogen oxides, and 4,900 tons of dust, compared with generating the same amount of electricity using **fossil fuels**.

The twenty wind generators of the Middelgrunden wind farm have been built in shallow water just off Copenhagen in Denmark.

Controversy

There is no doubt that **generating** electricity using wind power is very clean. However, many people are against this source of energy because of the large number of wind **turbines** that must be built in the countryside and off coastlines. People complain that wind farms are unattractive and noisy. In the past, wind farms did generate noise from the swishing of the blades and the hum of the gearbox. Modern designs, however, have eliminated most of the noise. Many people think that a wind farm makes a landscape more interesting, but there are just as many who think that a wind farm is unattractive.

There is considerable disturbance during the construction of a wind farm, with new access roads and the digging of foundations that extend many feet into the ground. Once constructed, the land around the turbines can be used as before, for livestock grazing for example. There is a possibility that the rotating blades could affect local bird populations, and in fact, there have been reports of birds being killed by the blades. However, some studies have shown that there is no measurable impact on birds.

In Britain, the government wants to increase the amount of electricity generated by **renewable** sources, including wind power, to ten percent. If all the wind turbines were built on land, an area of up to 2,316 square miles (6,000 square kilometers) would be needed for wind farms, and this would have a considerable effect on the landscape. Much of this land could still be used for farming because the the turbines themselves only occupy a fraction of this area. It is more likely, however, that the new wind farms will be built along the coast of the North Sea.

A row of wind turbines stretches across an attractive area of countryside in Anglesey in North Wales. Many people consider this wind farm to be intrusive and unattractive on the landscape.

Around the world

In the year 2000 alone, **3,800 megawatts** of new wind **energy generating** capacity was installed worldwide, most of which was in Europe. Germany has more than 9,000 wind **turbines** in operation. They produce three percent of the country's **electricity.** Germany is slowly getting rid of its nuclear power stations. The goal is to build enough wind farms each year to replace one nuclear power station. In Denmark, there are enough wind turbines to produce seventeen percent of its electricity.

Wind farms, such as this one on the vast open prairie land of Alberta, Canada, have been built around the world. The costs involved in using wind farms to generate electricity has been falling sharply.

There are also several wind farms under construction in Australia. These **renewable** energy projects are being developed in anticipation of new Australian legislation, which requires that 12.5 percent of the country's electricity comes from renewable energy sources by the year 2010.

Costs are tumbling. Large wind farms in the states of Texas, Iowa, and Minnesota are **generating** energy at about three cents per **kWh.** This compares very favorably with the costs of using natural gas to generate electricity. As gas prices increase, wind power could become the cheapest method of generating electricity.

In Costa Rica, there is a wind farm that produces electricity at between 5.5 and 7 cents per kWh. This is much cheaper than the local oil-fired power stations, which sell electricity at 13 cents per kWh.

The outlook for wind energy is extremely promising. It is becoming cheaper and more efficient. By 2020, more than ten percent of the world's electricity could come from wind power. It has the potential to provide developing countries with a clean source of electricity. It could provide insurance against the changing costs of oil and future shortages of **fossil fuels.** Wind energy will help countries reduce their emissions of greenhouse gases. A one-megawatt wind turbine, 164 to 197 feet (50 to 60 meters) tall, produces enough power to supply 300 homes. And every year it will save more than 2,000 tons of carbon dioxide, 12 tons of sulphur dioxide, and 8 tons of nitrogen oxides. It will generate enough energy to repay the energy used in its construction within just four months.

> *Wind energy is ready, today, to supply substantial amounts of electricity in the Empire State. The first New York wind projects are in place and operating well, and there is enough windy land for many more—enough to power nearly two million homes. Nationally, we believe that wind energy can provide six percent of U.S. electricity requirements by 2020. Governor Pataki's announcement, the largest state renewable energy procurement commitment in U.S. history, should give wind power a tremendous boost.*
> Randall Swisher, Executive Director,
> American Wind Energy Association, commenting
> on New York Governor George Pataki's
> decision to require state agencies to produce
> ten percent of electricity from renewable energy
> sources by 2005, and twenty percent by 2010

Trapping Light

The sun is a source of both light and heat **energy.** The heat energy can be used to heat air and water, while the light energy can be used to **generate electricity.** One of the major advantages of **solar power** is that this free source of energy can be used in remote locations.

Panels of photovoltaic cells, similar to those that circle this lighthouse off the coast of Guernsey in the Channel Islands, are a useful source of electricity in remote places.

Solar collectors

Solar collectors trap the sun's heat energy. A solar collector consists of a large, flat glass-covered box that contains a dark metal plate. The plate absorbs the heat, while the glass keeps the heat from escaping. Air or water flowing through a tube at the bottom of the box is warmed by the heat. Solar collectors are used to heat homes, provide hot water and air conditioning, produce salt, and turn saltwater into fresh drinking water in a process called desalination.

Photovoltaics

Solar cells, which use a technology known as photovoltaics, can convert light energy into electrical energy. Photovoltaic power systems were originally developed for use in space, where they could make use of a free source of energy—the sun. They still power most **satellites** circling Earth because they operate reliably for long periods and require virtually no maintenance.

Photovoltaic power systems do not burn fuel and have no moving parts, so they are clean and silent. This is especially important where the main alternatives for obtaining power and light in remote places are diesel **generators** and **kerosene** lanterns and candles. Once installed, photovoltaic power systems can operate continuously with little upkeep and low operating costs.

Photovoltaic cells are quite small, so they are easy to transport to remote places to produce electricity. For example, a few panels about three feet (one meter) in height are sufficient to power communications stations on mountaintops or navigational buoys at sea. Buildings can have special roofs made of photovoltaic panels, which generate electricity for use within the building. Photovoltaics can generate electricity to pump water, charge batteries, power road signs, and run weather stations. Tiny photovoltaic cells are found in some pocket calculators.

Large numbers of photovoltaic cells can be used together to generate substantial amounts of electricity. These cells on the roof of a solar-powered car supply its power.

Inside a cell

The most important parts of a **photovoltaic cell** are the thin layers of silicon inside it. Silicon is a **semiconductor.** When light hits the cell, electrical charges move between the layers and produce an electric **current.** The more light there is, the more **electricity** can be produced. There is a glass cover or similar transparent material that seals the cell and keeps rain out. A nonreflective coating prevents light from being reflected away from the cell.

The proportion of sunlight **energy** that the photovoltaic cell converts to electric energy is called conversion **efficiency.** Improving this efficiency is one way to make solar energy competitive with more traditional sources of energy. The first photovoltaic cells converted just one to two percent of sunlight energy into electric energy. The latest cells have a conversion efficiency of up to seventeen percent. This means they can be used in places where it is not sunny all the time.

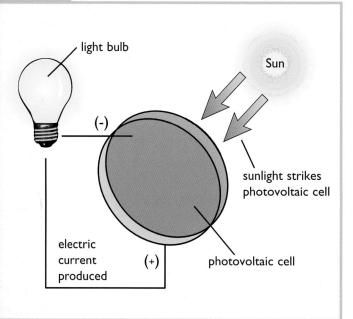

As more photovoltaic cells are manufactured, the costs of manufacturing them will come down. Already the latest photovoltaic cells are produced at a fraction of the cost of early photovoltaic systems. In time, the cost of producing electricity from photovoltaic cells will be competitive with the cost of electricity produced using **fossil fuels.**

The energy in sunlight is converted to electric energy by the photovoltaic cell. This can be used to power lights or electrical appliances.

There's an emerging market in the automobile industry—using photovoltaic products on the sunroof. A number of manufacturers are considering photovoltaics to ventilate a car—running a fan to keep the air moving when an auto sits in a parking lot.
John Corsi, Chief Executive Officer, Solarex

In 2001, NASA ran test flights on its Helios prototype. This unmanned flying wing runs on **solar power.** The entire top surface of the wing is covered with solar panels. Helios can cruise for days at altitudes three times higher than those used by commercial jets.

New research

Early photovoltaic cells consisted of a single crystal of pure silicon. The production of the crystals was very expensive. One of the latest developments in photovoltaic technology being researched is called Epilift. In the Epilift process, a silicon wafer is used as a production **template.** A semitransparent layer of high-quality silicon is laid on top of a template and then peeled off to produce solar cells. The original silicon wafer—the most expensive single item in solar panels—remains undamaged and can be used repeatedly. In addition to bringing the cost down, these cells have an energy conversion efficiency of up to twenty percent.

Solar power stations

Solar power stations have been built in sunny locations, such as California and Israel. There are two main types of solar power stations. Solar thermal power stations use sunlight to heat a fluid that in turn heats water to produce steam. Photovoltaic power stations use **photovoltaic cells** to convert sunlight into **electricity.**

Work started on the first solar thermal power station, Solar One, near Barstow, California, in the late 1970s. Electricity was first **generated** there in 1982. More than 1,800 mirrors were laid out in semicircles around a 256-foot (78-meter) tall tower. The mirrors directed sunlight onto a boiler at the top of the tower. As the sun moved through the sky, the mirrors followed it. Oil in the central collecting tower was heated and piped to a power plant. There, it heated water to 5,432°F (3,000°C) to produce steam. This was used to spin a **turbine,** which drove a **generator** to produce ten **kilowatts** of electricity.

Other power stations have mirrors shaped like feed troughs, that reflect sunlight onto a tube at the bottom. An example is the Luz station in California. A liquid inside the tube is heated by sunlight.

Unfortunately, large solar thermal power stations are expensive to build, and the costs per **megawatt** of solar **energy** cannot compete with other sources of energy. Thermal power stations must be built where there is plenty of sun, which may be far away from where the electricity is needed. This means that a power grid is needed to distribute the electricity. As a result, many of these power stations have become run down.

The first solar power stations were built in California, where the high number of sunny days made solar energy for large-scale electricity generation feasible.

Solar energy can be used as a source of heat for cooking and boiling water. The heat from these makeshift solar panels is used to boil water in this kettle in a remote mountain area of Tibet.

More recent solar power stations have used photovoltaic technology. The largest operating photovoltaic power station is in Italy. It generates 3.3 megawatts of electricity. In 1997 the Greek government approved the construction of the world's largest solar photovoltaic power station on the island of Crete. The solar power station will play an important role in the long-term plan of making Crete a solar-powered island. It is hoped that this proposed power station will generate 50 megawatts of electricity.

*The Mediterranean has a very high solar power potential, and the Crete example is a showcase for the region. It is the proof that our countries can be on the forefront of the solar power revolution and at the same time share the solution to **global warming.***
Dr. Mario Damato, Executive Director, Greenpeace Mediterranean

Redesigns

The White Cliffs **Solar Power** Station in Australia, which hasn't been used for more than five years, has recently undergone redevelopment. This solar thermal power station has been transformed to use the latest photovoltaic technology. The new plant uses the site and the reflector dishes of the old power station. There are fourteen huge, dish-shaped reflectors, that focus sunlight onto **photovoltaic cells.** These produce **electricity,** which enters the local power grid. When the project is complete, the White Cliffs Solar Power Station will have an output of 42 **kilowatts,** compared with the 25 kilowatts of the original solar thermal plant. This translates into 70,000 **kWh** of electricity per year, which is enough to make a significant contribution to the power needs of the area of White Cliffs.

Luz International

Luz International was a pioneering solar electric company in the United States during the 1980s. It completed its first solar power plant in 1985 in California's Mojave Desert. By 1991, Luz was generating 354 **megawatts** of solar electricity at nine adjoining sites. Although the company went out of business in 1992, its plants continue to produce electricity. During Luz's existence, the cost of solar electricity was cut from 25 cents per kWh to less than 8 cents. However, the solar power stations were not successful economically for several reasons. The natural gas prices and electricity costs did not rise as expected, while the operating and maintenance costs for the power stations did not fall as rapidly as had been expected. During the late 1980s, gas prices actually fell, bringing down the cost of electricity. Eventually Luz simply could not compete with the continuing decline of natural gas prices. Now the economic climate has changed. Gas prices have risen, and solar power prices are falling.

Orbiting solar power stations

Japan's Ministry of Economy, Trade, and Industry (METI) has announced plans to launch a giant solar power station by the year 2040. METI wants to launch a **satellite** capable of **generating** one million kilowatts per second, the equivalent to the output of a nuclear plant. The satellite would enter orbit about 22,370 miles (36,000 kilometers) above Earth's surface. It would have two huge solar power-generating wing panels.

Each panel would be 1.9 miles (3 kilometers) long, with one 3,282-foot (1,000-meter) diameter power transmission antenna between them. The electricity would be sent back to Earth in the form of microwaves. The receiving antenna on the ground, in a desert, or at sea would have a diameter of several miles. Then the electricity would be relayed along cables. The satellite is projected to weigh about 20,000 tons. The total construction cost is estimated at around two trillion yen (16.2 billion dollars). The estimated cost of generating power in space is high— about 23 yen (19 cents) per kilowatt hour, compared with 9 yen (7 cents) for thermal or nuclear power generation, but this may change as technology improves.

On Earth, clouds absorb sunlight, reducing (solar) power generation. But in space, we will be able to generate electric power even at night.
Osamu Takenouchi, METI

This is an artist's impression of a solar power station. The wings of this satellite would be covered with solar panels.

Water Power

Water can provide power in many different ways. Hydroelectric plans involve building a dam across a river to create a storage area for water. The water can be released through **turbines** to **generate electricity.** The power of the oceans, in the form of wave and tidal power, can also be harnessed to generate electricity.

Hydroelectric power

Today, hydroelectric power provides about ten percent of the world's electricity. It is a particularly important source of **energy** in mountainous areas and developing countries. The Itaipu Dam in Brazil is currently the largest hydroelectric power source in the world and can generate the same amount of power as twelve nuclear power stations. Not all dams, however, are used to generate electricity. The vast majority are built to provide water for irrigation and flood control.

Dams on rivers create reservoirs, or large lakes, that store water until it is needed. The stored water is released through pipes that lead to the turbines deep inside the dam. The falling water moves the turbines, which drive **generators.** The taller the dam, the farther the water falls, and the more electricity produced. When there is excess electricity, water can be pumped back up into the reservoir so that it can be released when there is a high electricity demand. Unlike other types of power generation, hydroelectric power is very efficient—about 90 percent of the water's energy is converted into electricity.

The Hoover Dam on the Colorado River supplies electricity to Las Vegas, which is rapidly expanding and using alot more energy.

The Three Gorges Dam—a good or bad thing?

The Three Gorges Dam is currently under construction. When complete, it will be the largest hydroelectric dam in the world, producing twice as much power as the Itaipu Dam in Brazil. It will create a reservoir 373 miles (600 kilometers) long. The dam's capacity will be 17 million **kilowatts,** and its projected annual power generation is 84 billion **kWh.** It will supply power mainly to central China. This project has attracted attention from around the world. It is a controversial project with many advantages and disadvantages. The advantages include:

- power generation. The dam will increase China's electricity output to ensure sufficient power for China's rapidly growing industries.
- flood prevention. The dam will prevent flooding, which in the past has killed thousands and left millions homeless.
- cleaner electricity. Hydroelectricity is cleaner than that produced by burning coal. Three-quarters of China's electricity comes from coal-fired power stations. The electricity from the project will reduce the need to burn more coal, which will reduce emissions of sulphur dioxide and carbon dioxide.

There are also a number of disadvantages to the project:

- It is estimated that the reservoir will partially or completely flood more than 262 square miles (600 square kilometers) of land, including two cities. More than one million people will have to be relocated.
- The dam and reservoir will alter the area's entire ecological system and environment. It will divert the river's natural course and flood hundreds of acres of land that is home to many species.
- Large quantities of silt will be dumped in the reservoir. Normally, the silt is dumped lower down the river, creating fertile flood plains.

The construction of the Three Gorges Dam on the Yangtze River near Chongqing in China is one of the world's largest engineering projects.

Wave energy

Winds blowing across the surface of the ocean create waves. The **energy** from the movement of the waves can be harnessed to produce **electricity.** There are two main types of wave energy generation devices: fixed and floating.

Fixed devices

Fixed **generating** devices are usually located on the seabed or the coast. One fixed device is called the Oscillating Water Column. Waves enter at the bottom of the column and force the air within the column through a **turbine.** Pressure increases within the column. As the wave retreats, the air is drawn back past the turbine due to the reduced air pressure on the ocean side of the turbine.

The TAPCHAN, or tapered channel system, is similar to the system used in hydroelectric power stations. It consists of a channel connected to a reservoir in a cliff. This channel gets steadily narrower,

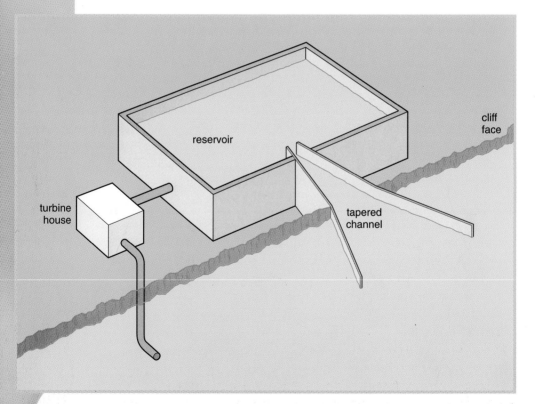

reservoir

cliff face

turbine house

tapered channel

A TAPCHAN system can only be used where there are consistent waves and a tidal range of less than three feet (one meter).

A prototype wave-power **generator** was installed on the coast of Islay, Scotland, in 2000. As water enters and leaves a partly submerged chamber, the air above the water is compressed (squeezed) and decompressed. The forced air then drives a turbine. This generator can produce enough electricity to supply local villages.

causing the waves to increase in height. Eventually, the waves are high enough to pour over the walls into the reservoir. Then the stored water in the reservoir is fed through a turbine. Unfortunately, TAPCHAN systems are not suitable for all coastal regions. The ideal location is one with consistent waves, good wave energy, and a tidal range of less than three feet (one meter).

Floating devices

Floating wave energy devices generate electricity when they rise and fall with the motion of waves. One design consists of ten floating tubes placed end to end, forming a flexible tube 394 feet (120 meters) long. Each tube moves up and down independently. Its movement drives pumps that produce electricity. There have been a number of different designs including Salter Duck, Clam, and the Archimedes Wave Swing. All have had limited success, but none has been used commercially.

35

The tidal barrage across the River Rance in France generates **electricity** for local towns. There is a 26-foot (8-meter) difference in height between low and high tide.

Tidal energy

A tidal barrage is a huge damlike structure built across an **estuary,** with a series of **sluice gates** and **turbines** at the base. When the tide rises, the water fills the estuary and pushes through the turbines. It then becomes trapped behind the dam. When the tide falls, the water passes through in the opposite direction, turning the turbines again.

There are a number of barrages around the world. The Rance barrage in France makes use of a 26-foot (8-meter) tidal range and can **generate** eleven **gigawatts.** The barrage built in the Bay of Fundy in Canada has a range of up to 53 feet (16 meters) and can generate 29 gigawatts. There are also large barrages off the coast of China, which were built to replace coal-fired power stations.

Environmental damage

Dams built across a river or an estuary and tidal barrages have severe environmental implications, as they interfere with the flow of water.

Dams on rivers create reservoirs that flood large areas of land. For example, the Balbina Dam in Brazil flooded 926 square miles (2,400 square kilometers) of rain forest. Water entering the reservoir dumps its silt, and this causes a buildup of silt in the reservoir, which eventually has to be dredged. Normally, this silt would be dumped on the river's flood plain, providing a source of nutrients for the soil.

Lake Moogerah in Queensland, Australia, was created by damming a river. The newly formed lake has flooded a rain forest. The remains of the trees can still be seen.

The capacity of Lake Nasser behind the Aswan Dam on the River Nile in Egypt has been severely reduced by silt. Downstream of the dam the river transports less than ten percent of its normal load of silt. This means that less silt reaches the Nile Delta, which is now being eroded. In addition, Nile Valley farmers must increasingly rely on artificial fertilizers instead of silt.

Silt increases the nutrient content of the water. Algae use the nutrients and rapidly increase in number, producing an algal bloom over the surface of the water. As the algae die, they are decomposed by bacteria. This increases the number of bacteria, which use up the oxygen in the water. The lack of oxygen causes fish and other organisms in the water to die.

Pros and cons

Tidal barrages also have a number of environmental consequences. They reduce the tidal range so that there are no extreme low or high tides. Low-lying mud flats and salt marshes could become permanently flooded, resulting in a loss of habitat for wading birds, which are abundant in estuarine areas. The flush time—the time it takes for water to move out of the estuary—could increase, causing **pollutants** in the water to remain there for longer before draining out and being diluted in the open sea. The salt concentration could decrease and harm marine organisms. However, some biologists believe that some of these changes could lead to an increase in the different types of invertebrate species. There would be more food for birds, although the birds may be different from those that are there now. Hence, there are many pros and cons associated with tidal barrages.

Heat from the Ground

The earth is still cooling from the time it was formed, and its **core** is similar to an **energy** store. **Geothermal** power uses energy **generated** from within the earth's core. In volcanic areas, such as Iceland, New Zealand, and parts of the United States, hot rocks lie close to the earth's surface. The heat warms the surface waters, creating hot springs. In addition, the sun heats the surface layers of the ground.

New Zealand's North Island has several hot springs such as this one, Whakarewarewa Thermal Reserve. The hot springs have been created by water passing hot rocks before coming to the surface.

Tapping the hot water

Geothermal heat can be used in two ways. One method is simply to pump out the hot water and use it to heat buildings or to produce steam to generate **electricity.** Geothermal power stations are built close to hot springs, so they can use the natural sources of steam to spin their **turbines.** The world's largest geothermal power station is The Geysers, near San Francisco. This power station can produce much of the electricity needed by the city. More than 250 wells have been drilled into the rocks, and they carry steam directly from the ground into the power station. Some of the deepest wells reach nearly 2.5 miles (4 kilometers) into the earth. In modern geothermal plants, once the water has cooled down it is pumped back into the ground to replace the water that was extracted. The water is reheated by the hot rocks near the earth's surface.

The second method is to pump cold water through a bore hole into hot rocks that are highly fractured. The cold water seeps through the cracks in these hot rocks and is heated by them. Then, the hot water is pumped up to the surface through a second bore hole. Prototypes have been built, but this method has not been used on a commercial scale. One of the problems is figuring out how to prevent a high-pressure, high-temperature **blowout.**

The waste water from this Icelandic geothermal power station is still quite warm. It is used to heat the Blue Lagoon, a recreational pool popular with bathers.

Environmental impact

Although **geothermal energy** is a very clean energy source, it must be used properly to prevent possible environmental damage. New geothermal systems re-inject water into the earth after its heat is used. This preserves the resource and contains the gases and heavy metals that are sometimes found in geothermal fluids. Care must be taken in planning geothermal projects to ensure that they do not cool nearby hot springs or cause intermixing with ground water. Geothermal projects can produce some carbon dioxide emissions, but these are a fraction of those produced by the cleanest **fossil fuel** power plants of the same size.

In Iceland, underground heating pipes along the streets ensure that the roads are ice-free all year. Here, new heating pipes are being laid in a street in the capital city, Reykjavik.

Ground heat

The temperature of the ground is remarkably constant all year round. Although there may be temperature variations in the top layer of soil, deeper down the temperature stays the same all year, approximately 43°F (6°C). Ground heat pumps can be used to provide heating and air conditioning in homes. These pumps are highly efficient and make use of the temperature difference between the air and the ground. In the winter, heat is removed from the ground and transferred into a building for heating. In the summer, heat is removed from the building to provide air conditioning or cooling and pumped into the ground. On either cycle, water is heated for washing, cooking, and so on.

The heat pump unit takes the place of a boiler inside the home or building. In a typical installation, a loop of plastic pipe is placed in a nearby vertical drill hole that may reach down 99 feet (30 meters) or more. Then the hole is filled with clay. A water-antifreeze solution is circulated through the loop and the heat pump. In winter, a cold solution passes along the pipe and picks up heat from the ground. When it enters the house again, it is several degrees warmer. In summer, the hot air in the house heats the solution, which enters the loop in the ground where it loses its heat. A cooler solution then returns to the house. More than 100,000 heat pumps have been installed in buildings in the United States.

We've had a fourfold increase in interest [in geothermal systems] over the past four years. . . . Prices vary, but for economy of operation, geothermal wins hands down.

Duwayne Marks, Director of Energy Efficiency
Virginia Power

Nuclear Energy

Nuclear power is produced by splitting atoms, not by burning fuel. All matter is made up of tiny particles called atoms. Each atom consists of a **nucleus** made of protons and neutrons surrounded by electrons. When the nucleus of a large atom splits in two, **energy** is released. This is called nuclear fission. There are currently more than 400 nuclear power stations around the world. Together, they **generate** approximately sixteen percent of the world's **electricity.** Nuclear power generation is clean, but there are major concerns about its safety and cost. The fuel source is the metal uranium. Only a tiny amount is needed because 15.5 ounces (500 grams) of this metal produces the same quantity of heat as 1,400 tons of coal.

Fission reactions

The uranium atom is large and unstable. Its instability means that neutrons are given off by the nucleus. These neutrons move fast and may bump into other uranium atoms, causing them to split and release heat energy. This sets off a chain reaction, with nucleus after nucleus splitting. When this occurs, vast amounts of energy are released. But this chain reaction has to be controlled or a massive explosion will result. This is exactly what happened in early atomic bombs. Fission reactions can be controlled if some of the neutrons are absorbed.

The nuclear reactor

Nuclear fission takes place inside a **reactor** that is surrounded by a thick layer of concrete or steel. One of the more advanced designs for a nuclear power station is the advanced gas-cooled reactor. The uranium is spread out in thin fuel rods and lowered into the reactor. Control rods are between the fuel rods. They are made of a material called boron, which absorbs neutrons. By lowering and raising the control rods, it is possible to control the chain reaction. If the control rods are lowered, more neutrons are absorbed and the chain reaction slows down. Both the fuel and control rods are surrounded by a moderator. This is a substance, such as graphite, that does not change during the reactions, but helps to slow down the neutrons. Carbon dioxide gas is pumped around the reactor to take up heat from the reaction within the reactor. The hot carbon dioxide is used to heat water to produce steam.

Is nuclear power safe?

There are major problems with nuclear power. When uranium atoms split, they produce smaller particles, which are **radioactive.** These radioactive particles can cause cancer and even death. Therefore, the thick layer of concrete or lead around the reactor is essential to prevent these particles from entering the environment. However, once the uranium is used up, the fuel rods have to be replaced. Used fuel rods are highly radioactive, as are the control rods. The reactor has a life of up to 50 years, after which time it can no longer be used. Careful disposal is needed for all of these radioactive materials, but there are no guaranteed safe disposal methods. These materials are so dangerous that they have to be buried in special containers in the ground for hundreds of years.

Another risk is the threat from radiation leakage during an accident. A major nuclear accident occurred at the Chernobyl nuclear reactor in the Ukraine on April 26, 1986. Two explosions produced a huge radioactive cloud that spread across Europe. To prevent further leaks, the entire reactor plant was encased in concrete (shown right). Since that time, more than 125,000 people may have died prematurely as a result of exposure to Chernobyl radiation. High-energy radioactive particles can pass deep into the body, where they damage or kill cells. Exposure to a large dose of radiation will kill a large number of cells. The long-term damage can include cancer. Cancer is caused by cells dividing uncontrollably. This abnormal growth of cells is called a tumor. Damage to cells in the reproductive system can cause birth defects in children, such as missing limbs and brain damage.

Nuclear fusion

A process called nuclear fusion powers the sun. The high temperature of the sun causes small **nuclei** to collide into each other with such force that they fuse to form one heavier nucleus. At the same time, **energy** is released.

Scientists are hoping that the next generation of nuclear power stations will be powered by nuclear fusion. The fuel will be heavy hydrogen, called deuterium, and the waste material will be water. When two nuclei of heavy hydrogen fuse, their combined masses are slightly less than the mass of the original particles. This tiny amount represents the energy. The energy can be harnessed and used to **generate electricity.**

The problem is that the fuel has to be heated to temperatures of up to 212 million°F (100 million°C) and has to be contained by very powerful magnets. Scientists have built small prototype **reactors** and have even managed to make the nuclei fuse. But it only worked for a few seconds and used far more energy than was released by the fusion. To make electricity commercially, a fusion reactor will have to work consistently for decades. Although fusion reactors will solve many of the world's energy problems, a commercial reactor will probably not be available for many decades, and the costs will be high.

The experimental Tokamak reactor has powerful magnets. These create a magnetic field that squeezes hot **plasma** into a very small space. This brings the deuterium and tritium (another heavy form of hydrogen) together so they can fuse.

The hydrogen bomb

The atomic bombs that fell on Japan at the end of World War II were based on the fission reaction. Atomic bombs contain uranium or plutonium, which is split to release vast amounts of energy and **radioactive** particles. The hydrogen bomb, also known as a thermonuclear bomb, is different. It relies on the fusion reaction, and its fuel is a special form of hydrogen. The fusion reaction begins when hydrogen is subjected to extremely high temperatures. The explosion of a hydrogen bomb creates an extremely hot zone near its center, which **vaporizes** nearly all matter present to form a gas at extremely high pressure. Then, a destructive shock wave travels outward. Extremely high temperatures are required to start a fusion reaction. The high temperatures are created by the explosion of a small fission bomb, so a small amount of radioactivity is released. Scientists are trying to control this type of fusion reaction in a fusion reactor.

The first thermonuclear explosion took place in 1952 at Eniwetok Atoll in the South Pacific. The explosion created a classic mushroom cloud above the island.

Bioenergy

Each year, plants trap enough **energy** to meet the world's energy demands up to eight times over. But only a fraction of this energy is utilized. Plants represent a **renewable** source of energy. Wood is the world's oldest and most common form of **bioenergy.** The supply of wood can be maintained if more trees are planted after they are harvested. However, in many parts of the developing world, wood is being burned faster than it is being replaced. Fortunately, there are many other plants that can be grown on a large scale to provide energy.

Biofuels

Biofuels are produced either from plants that are grown especially for fuel, or from plant wastes. Straw is left over after harvesting cereal crops. This waste can be used as a fuel in power stations. In Denmark, this source of energy provides 1.5 percent of the country's energy needs.

Energy crops are plants grown just to **generate** energy. The plants, such as willow, sugar cane, bananas, and *Miscanthus* (a tall bamboo-like grass), are fast-growing and can be harvested within a short time. Their energy content is approximately half that of coal and one-third

Willow is a fast-growing plant. It is left to grow for four or five years, then the shoots are cut down to ground level and allowed to regrow.

that of oil. Grasses are harvested annually, while willow is harvested at intervals of four or five years. Sugar cane and *Miscanthus* grow to heights of up to ten feet (three meters) in a single season. The woody stems are harvested at the end of the growing season, and new shoots appear the following spring. Willow plants are cut down to a stump and left to regrow. Approximately 99 acres (40 hectares) of willow will generate power for thousands of homes.

Designer oil crops

Many industrial oils are derived from **fossil fuels** or from expensive chemical processes. In the future, oil crops may be genetically modified to give them the ability to make oils that have particular industrial uses. This involves finding a gene responsible for making a particular oil in an organism, removing the gene from the organism's **DNA,** and inserting it into the DNA of the crop plant. The crop will then be able to make specific oils. For example, petroselinic acid is a compound used in the manufacture of plastics, detergents, and nylon. The coriander plant produces this substance. However, it is not possible to grow coriander as an oil crop. If the gene that makes this compound in coriander can be identified, it could be transferred to the oil seed rape plant. Oil seed rape could then be grown and processed for this chemical, rather than for food oils.

Genetic engineering could make the oil seed rape plant produce oils suitable for industrial use.

Powering cars

Many plants produce oils that can be used to fuel cars. This fuel is called biodiesel. Different oil crops around the world can be used, such as oil seed rape in Europe and North America, coconut oil in the Philippines, sunflower oil in South Africa, and palm and castor oil in Brazil.

Another fuel derived from plants is ethanol. Ethanol is produced from crops such as sugar cane and sugar beet, corn, and even organic wastes. The Clean Air Act of 1990 requires that gas sold in polluted cities be at least two percent oxygen by weight. The oxygen ensures complete **combustion** of the fuel when it burns, especially when the engine is cold. It also reduces the levels of **pollutants** such as carbon monoxide. Gas is modified by adding either six percent ethanol by volume or eleven percent of an additive called MTBE. For a while MTBE was the preferred option of the oil companies. But recently it was discovered that MTBE is contaminating water sources across the United States. It is soluble in water and once in water it breaks down very slowly. Now there is a growing interest in ethanol as a fuel.

Sugar cane is a fast-growing crop. This sugar from a plantation in Hawaii could be harvested for use in the production of ethanol.

Gasohol is another fuel that contains ethanol. Gasohol is 80 to 90 percent gasoline and 10 to 20 percent ethanol. A gallon of gasohol produces less air pollution than a gallon of gasoline. Gasohol makes up 24 percent of the market in Brazil. Sugar cane is grown extensively in Brazil, so there is a ready supply of ethanol. Unfortunately, gasohol costs more than regular gasoline and has to be subsidized.

The ethanol plants of today will be the biorefineries of tomorrow. The days of big oil are coming to an end.

Jim Evangelow, Chemical
Strategies, New York

Gas stations in Brazil sell a range of fuels, including gasohol. Gasohol produces fewer air pollutants than the equivalent amount of gasoline.

Biogas

Biogas is a gas that is produced when animal and plant wastes rot. Bacteria ferment the waste under anaerobic, or oxygen-free, conditions. The products of this fermentation include carbon dioxide and methane.

Methane is produced in landfills, where the buried waste decays and **generates** this gas. Often, methane is allowed to escape into the atmosphere. However, it could be collected and piped to local industries where it could be burned to release heat.

Biogas can also be produced under more controlled conditions in pits in the ground or in tanks called biogas digesters. All forms of human and animal waste can be put into the digester. The rotting mass releases gases, such as methane, that can be piped away and burned as a fuel for heating and cooking.

A wide range of waste materials, such as animal dung, can be put into a biogas digester. The resulting gas can be used for heating and cooking in the home.

Biogas is a major fuel in many developing countries, where almost every rural family or village could make use of a biogas digester to generate fuel. Biogas digesters can be used on farms to dispose of animal wastes. The biogas can be used to power a **generator** to produce **electricity.** The intensive farming practiced in Denmark and the Netherlands generates large amounts of animal waste, which needs careful disposal. It is fermented in digesters to produce biogas, while the residue is used as fertilizer.

Elsewhere, household wastes, livestock waste, and poultry waste are burned in specially modified power stations, rather than used to make biogas. These power stations have to meet strict emission controls to prevent the release of toxic chemicals.

This biogas power plant near Bergen in Norway runs on methane collected from landfill waste disposal sites.

The Future of Renewable Sources

Today, alternative **energy** sources represent only fifteen percent of all energy uses. Most of this comes from biofuels. Only a small percentage comes from wind and solar energy. This will have to change. In the future, it is likely that this figure will be reversed, with alternative energy sources providing 85 percent of the energy, and **fossil fuels** only 15 percent. The alternative energy sources will need to conform to the increasingly strict emission requirements of many countries.

New technological developments will be needed to be sure that the energy conversions are as efficient as possible. In addition to the sources already identified in this book, it will be necessary to find other sources. One source that has been mostly ignored is deep water.

Looking to the ocean

The oceans cover two-thirds of our planet's surface. They range in depth from just a few feet near the coast to several miles in depth. Many of the deeper parts of the ocean have not yet been explored.

Vast underwater kelp forests are found off the California coast. These seaweeds grow rapidly and could be used as a source of energy.

Forests of seaweed lie In the shallow waters off many coasts and are a potential source of energy. Harvesting seaweed is not a new concept. It is used as a food, fed to animals, and spread on fields as a natural fertilizer. But it is not yet used as a fuel. Fast-growing seaweeds called kelp can be grown as a crop and then harvested. Giant kelp can grow up to three feet (one meter) in height each day. In a trial experiment, kelp was farmed in the sea off California. It was harvested and used to make methane gas. Kelp digesters that produce methane may one day become common in many coastal towns around the world.

Ocean thermal energy conversion

Within the 30-degree latitude on either side of the equator, there is a thermocline in the ocean. This means there is a temperature difference between the water at the surface and at depths of 3,282 feet (1,000 meters). The temperature of the surface layer of water is 77°F (25°C), while the water at 3,282 feet (1,000 meters) is only 41°F (5°C). The warm surface water can be used to evaporate liquids with a low boiling point, such as chlorofluorocarbons (CFCs) and ammonia. This produces a vapor that can be used to drive a **turbine** attached to a **generator.** Cold seawater passing through a condenser turns the vapor back to liquid to restart the system.

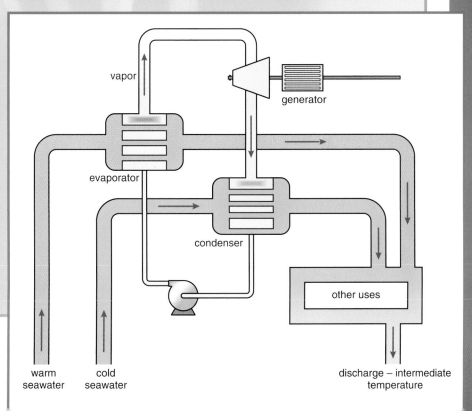

Tidal barrages and underwater wind farms

Tidal barrages can be an effective way to **generate** power, and there are many sites in the world where they could be built. One of the best sites in the world is the Severn Estuary in Britain. Although there is a plan to develop a barrage across the **estuary,** it has not yet been approved. However, large tidal barrages have a harmful effect on the wildlife in an estuary. Instead, engineers are now studying the powerful underwater currents that run along many coasts.

Offshore wind farms, such as the new Middelgrunden wind farm, are built in shallow waters, so the **turbines** are still above the water. In the future, wind **generators** could disappear under the sea. These underwater wind farms would be built in places where the currents are strong. The flow of water, not wind, would turn the blades and power the turbine. Potentially, a single turbine could produce enough power to supply a small village. And, water currents are far more reliable than the wind. But the turbines cannot be placed just anywhere. They need to be located in places where there is deep water to cover the blades; but near to the shore, so that the cables carrying the **electricity** are short; and away from shipping routes and areas of nature conservation.

Today, grain silos, such as these in Nebraska, are built close to the fields where cereal crops grow. In the future, the silos could be replaced by biorefineries that will process the crops.

Marine methane

Scientists have discovered that there is enough methane gas lying on the seabed to keep the world supplied with **energy** for hundreds of years. This methane was produced by bacteria feeding on the remains of dead plants and animals. The cold waters of the deep ocean caused the methane to freeze, and it now lies scattered in tiny crystals over the seabed. But accessing this source of energy is difficult. One way to collect the methane may be to pump steam down a pipe onto the seabed. The heat would melt the crystals, turning the methane back to gas. The gas could then be trapped in an underwater balloon and towed by submarine to docks for storage. The methane, however, is a kind of **fossil fuel,** and therefore, is not a **renewable** source of energy.

Biorefineries

Today, oil refineries take crude oil and break it down into parts that can then be used for a wide range of materials, including plastics. In the future, much more use will have to be made of plants. The oil refineries could be replaced by "green" biorefineries. Instead of oil, crops would be processed into plastics, chemicals, and fuels. One grain manufacturer in Nebraska has already built a factory where crops go in and a whole range of products come out, including polyactic acid, which is used in plastics for clothing, food containers, and film. "Green" plastics may be made from corn and wheat, while oil seed rape and soybeans could be used to make biogas.

Mobile power

Fuel cells will play an increasingly important role in storing and releasing energy. However, the current models are heavy and bulky. Research is under way to produce tiny fuel cells that will be small enough to power laptops and cell phones. These fuel cells will have to be light, easy to recharge, and last a long time. The goal is to produce a fuel cell that runs for twelve hours and can be recharged with a small amount of liquid fuel.

The most promising design is the direct methanol fuel cell, which runs on a mix of two percent methanol in water. First, the methanol is converted to carbon dioxide and hydrogen. Normally this reaction takes place only at high temperatures. However, the presence of a platinum **catalyst** allows the reaction to take place at low temperatures. Then the hydrogen reacts with oxygen. The use of platinum makes the cell expensive but allows the use of a liquid fuel.

Conclusion

It is clear that people will continue to burn **fossil fuels** as long as they are available. Fortunately, there will be less pollution from burning these fuels due to the use of anti-pollution technology. But in the future, many new sources of **energy** will be needed. They will have to both replace the fossil fuels and supply the extra energy needs of a growing world population.

Growing demands

The world's population is growing rapidly, especially in the developing world. Countries such as China and India are developing economically, and their people have greater wealth. This leads to higher standards of living and more people will own cars. All of this will increase energy demands even further. Energy demands in wealthy industrial countries continue to grow. The United States already uses more power than any other country, and its energy requirements are steadily increasing. The U.S. Department of Energy estimates that if energy demands in the United States continue to increase at the current rate, there will be a need for an extra 1,000 power stations by the year 2020. However, a program of energy **efficiency** measures could reduce this requirement to 600 power stations. Such measures could include legislation that electrical appliances, especially air-conditioning units, must be more energy efficient. Also, households could replace traditional light bulbs with energy efficient ones, and new building standards could improve the heating efficiency of homes and offices.

These Australian **solar-powered** hot water cylinders provide a high-tech solution to a household need.

Best alternative

As fossil fuels become more rare, governments may look again at nuclear energy. Nuclear fission will still be at the heart of many nuclear power stations, but developments in technology mean that these power stations will be much safer than current designs. Within 50 years it is also possible that the first commercial fusion power station could be in operation.

However, there is a better option—**fuel cells.** These can be compared to a highly efficient engine with no moving parts. Wherever power is used, fuel cells can be used as an alternative, from powering cell phones and laptops to **generating electricity** on a commercial scale. Potentially, fuel cells could replace every battery and **combustion** engine in the world. At the moment, fuel cells are expensive, costing thousands of dollars per **kilowatt** of power, compared with $44 per kilowatt for a car engine and $585 per kilowatt for a gas **turbine** power plant. However, once the cells are produced in large quantities, the price will fall, and in time the costs will be comparable with and possibly cheaper than conventional power sources. Engineers will have to redesign things such as cars in order to use fuel cells. It is even possible that one day everyone may have their own personal power plant, based on a fuel cell that provides all their needs for powering cars and homes.

Energy crisis

At the moment, most electricity is supplied by large, central power stations that feed electricity into a national power grid. Often the fossil fuels are imported. These power stations cause more pollution and are less efficient than some of the newer energy sources. People will have to learn to depend on a variety of energy sources, with each source generating energy on a small scale. Advances in energy technology are being made all the time, but some scientists argue that there will come a time when the demand for energy outstrips the supply.

> *Within five years I'll be able to go down to Wal-Mart and pick a microgenerator off the shelf to power my house. I will take it home and connect it to the gas pipe. It will generate power as well as heat my house and produce hot water. And it will be much cheaper than using the power grid.*
>
> Karl Yeager, Electric Power Research Institute in California

Timeline

1500– 1600	The Dutch improve on the design of windmills and use the new design for grinding grain.
1767	Swiss scientist Horace de Saussure builds the world's first solar collector, which is used by Sir John Herschel to cook food during his expedition to South Africa in the 1830s.
1839	Sir William Grove, a British scientist, writes the first known account of the **fuel cell.**
1854	A wind-powered water pump is introduced in the United States. It is a fan type, with many **vanes** around a wheel and a tail to keep it pointed into the wind.
1891	U.S. inventor Clarence Kemp patents the first commercial solar water heater.
1895	Two businessmen buy the rights to Kemp's solar system and, with the help of high gas and coal prices, fit 30 percent of homes in Pasadena, CA with solar water heating systems by 1897.
1908	William Bailey of the Carnegie Steel Company invents a solar collector with an insulated box and copper coils. By the end of World War II, more than 4,000 have been sold. The number increases to 60,000 units by 1941.
1940	More than six million wind-powered water pumps are being used in the United States, mainly for pumping water and **generating electricity**.
1941	A 1.25-**megawatt** wind **turbine** is hooked to the Central Vermont Public Service grid near Rutland, Vermont.
1942	The first experimental nuclear power station is built at the University of Chicago. Denmark links a 200-**kilowatt** wind turbine to its national power grid.
1952	The first hydrogen bomb is exploded in Eniwetok in the South Pacific by the United States.
1954	Bell Telephone researchers discover the sensitivity of a silicon wafer to sunlight, and the solar cell is developed.

1956   The first commercial nuclear power station opens at Calder Hall in Britain.

1973   Oil prices rise dramatically. There are further shortages when Arab oil exporting countries set up an oil **embargo.** The oil shortages persuade governments to set up programs to develop alternative **energy** sources, such as wind and **solar power.** In the United States, Westinghouse Electric receives a Department of Energy/NASA contract to develop first-generation 200-kilowatt wind turbines.

1982   The world's first **solar power** station, Solar One, near Barstow, California, starts generating electricity.

1981–   California tax credits lead to the commercial
1984   development of wind power in California. During this period 6,870 turbines are installed.

1986   The cost of wind power is approximately nine and a half cents per **kWh**.

1990   In the United States, the Clean Air Act of 1990 requires gasoline sold in polluted cities to be at least two percent oxygen by weight.

1994   The cost of wind power falls to below three and a half cents, making it competitive with many other power **generators**.

1995   More than 1.2 million buildings in the United States have solar water heating systems, and there are 250,000 solar-heated swimming pools.

2000   More than 3,800 megawatts of new wind energy generating capacity are brought online worldwide. The global wind power capacity rises to 17,300 megawatts, enough to generate some 37 billion kWh of electricity each year. Several of the world's largest wind farms approach completion in the United States. Four wind farms of 200 megawatts are installed in Texas, California, and the Pacific Northwest. An extra 2,000 megawatts of wind energy will be available in the United States.

2001   The costs of generating electricity from some of the latest U.S. wind farms falls to less than two and a half cents per kWh. This power source is now more affordable than natural gas. Californians experience major power shortages. The world's largest offshore wind farm opens near Copenhagen, Denmark.

Glossary

acid rain rain that contans air pollutants like nitrogen oxides and sulfur oxides

bioenergy **energy** derived from plants, such as wood, grasses, or sugar cane

blowout sudden explosion of oil or water from the ground

catalyst chemical that enables reactions to take place more readily or at lower temperatures

combustion burning

composite material made of two or more substances

condense to change from gas or vapor to liquid

core central part

current flow or movement of electrically charged particles

DNA deoxyribonucleic acid, genetic material found in most cells

efficiency measure of how much energy is usefully transferred as the form of energy you want

electricity form of energy made up of charged particles that flow along a conductor creating an electric current

electrochemical chemistry that involves electricity

electrode conductor through which electricity enters or leaves a substance. It is usually a wire or rod.

electrolyte substance that conducts electricity when molten or in a solution such as acidified water

electromagnet soft iron core that is made into a magnet when electricity flows through a surrounding coil

embargo order by a government that prevents commercial activity

energy power, such as heat, electricity, or movement

estuary place where a river enters the sea and fresh water meets saltwater

exhaust hot gases emitted by an engine of a vehicle

flywheel heavy wheel on a spinning shaft used to control machinery or store energy

fossil fuel fuel that forms in the earth over million of years from the remains of dead plants and animals. Coal, oil, and gas are fossil fuels.

fuel cell device that converts energy. Electricity and heat are produced when the fuels within a fuel cell react together.

generate produce

generator device that produces electrical energy

geothermal energy from the earth's hot core

gigawatt 1,000,000,000 watts

global warming process by which the average global temperature of the earth is gradually increasing

impermeable something that cannot be penetrated

kerosene type of fuel derived from oil such as paraffin oil

kilowatt 1,000 watts

kinetic energy energy an object has because it is moving

kWh kilowatt hour

megawatt one million watts

nucleus (plural **nuclei**) central part of an atom made up of protons and neutrons

pH measure of how acidic something is

photovoltaic cell/panel solar cell that can convert light energy into electricity using silicon. Many cells can be positioned together to form a panel.

plasma gas of protons and neutrons

pollutant substance that contaminates the air, land, or water

radioactive property of a substance, giving off subatomic particles

reactor place in a nuclear power station where nuclear fission takes place

renewable describes energy sources that are naturally replaced and will not run out

satellite artificial body placed in orbit around the earth

semiconductor solid substance that does not conduct electricity at low temperatures but becomes more conductive at higher temperatures

sluice gate sliding gate that controls the flow or volume of water

smog layer of fog and smoke mixed with air pollutants that hangs over a city

solar power energy derived from the sun

template pattern used to guide the manufacture of something

turbine machine used to change movement energy into mechanical energy

vane blade of a wind generator

vaporize to turn a liquid into a gas

Further Reading

McLeish, Ewan. *Energy Resources: Our Impact on the Planet.* Austin, Tex.: Raintree/Steck Vaughn, 2002.

Miller, Kimberly M. *What If We Run Out of Fossil Fuels?* Danbury, Conn.: Children's Press, 2002.

Parker, Steve. *Earth's Resources.* Austin, Tex.: Raintree/Steck Vaughn, 2001.

Index